I0087423

A CourseGuide for

How to Read the Bible for All Its Worth

Gordon D. Fee
Douglas Stuart
Mark L. Strauss

**ZONDERVAN
ACADEMIC**

ZONDERVAN ACADEMIC

A CourseGuide for How to Read the Bible for All Its Worth

Copyright © 2020 by Zondervan

Requests for information should be addressed to:
Zondervan, *3900 Sparks Dr. SE, Grand Rapids, Michigan 49546*

ISBN 978-0-310-11018-7 (softcover)

CONTENTS

Introduction 5

1. Introduction: The Need to Interpret 7

2. The Basic Tool: A Good Translation 11

3. The Epistles: Learning to Think Contextually 15

4. The Epistles: The Hermeneutical Question 19

5. The Old Testament Narratives: Their Proper Use 23

6. Acts: The Question of Historical Precedent 27

7. The Gospels: One Story, Many Dimensions 31

8. The Parables: Do You Get the Point? 35

9. The Law(s): Covenant Stipulations for Israel 39

10. The Prophets: Enforcing the Covenant in Israel 44

11. The Psalms: Israel's Prayers and Ours 48

12. Wisdom: Then and Now 52

13. Revelation: Images of Judgment and Hope 56

Introduction

Welcome to *A CourseGuide for How to Read the Bible for All Its Worth*. These guides were created for formal and informal students alike who want to engage deeper in biblical, theological, or ministry studies. We hope this guide will provide an opportunity for you to grow not only in your understanding, but also in your faith.

How to Use This Guide

This guide is meant to be used in conjunction with the book *How to Read the Bible for All Its Worth* and its corresponding videos, *How to Read the Bible for All Its Worth Video Lectures*. After you have read each chapter in the book and watched the accompanying video lesson, the materials in this guide will help you review and assess what you have learned. Application-oriented questions are included as well.

Each CourseGuide has been individually designed to best equip you in your studies, but in general, you can expect the following components. Most CourseGuides begin every chapter with a "You Should Know" section, which highlights key terminology, people, and facts to remember. This section serves as a helpful summary for directing your studies. Reflection questions, typically two to three per chapter, prompt you to summarize key points you've learned. Discussion questions invite you to an even deeper level of engagement. Finally, most chapters will end with a short quiz to test your retention. You can find the answer key to each quiz at the bottom of the page following it.

For Further Study

CourseGuides accompany books and videos from some of the world's top biblical and theological scholars. They may be used independently, or in small groups or classrooms, offering quality instruction to equip students for academic and ministry pursuits. If you would like to engage in further study with Zondervan's CourseGuides, the full lineup may be viewed online. After completing your studies with *A CourseGuide for How to Read the Bible for All Its Worth*, we recommend moving on to *A CourseGuide for Grasping God's Word* and *A Course-Guide for Introduction to Biblical Interpretation*.

CHAPTER 1

Introduction: The Need to Interpret

You Should Know

- Translation is interpretation.
- A text cannot mean what it could never have meant for its original readers/hearers.
- The Bible: the Word of God given in human words in history
- Aim of good interpretation: "plain meaning of the text"
- Two levels of interpretation: exegesis; hermeneutics
- Exegesis: careful, systematic study of the Scripture to discover the original, intended meaning
- First step in interpreting the Bible: exegesis
- Historical context: the time and culture of the author and audience
- Literary context: Words only have meaning in sentences; biblical sentences have meaning in relation to surrounding sentences; asks, "What's the point?"; traces the author's train of thought
- Hermeneutics: seeking the contemporary relevance of the Bible; asking questions about the Bible's meaning in the "here and now"

Essay Questions

Short

1. The key to good exegesis and a more intelligent reading of the Bible is to learn to read it carefully and to ask the right questions of the text. How does one read it carefully, and what are those "right questions"?

2. Why is the question "what's the point?" the most important contextual question you will ask of the Bible?

3. "A text cannot mean what it could never have meant for its original readers/hearers." What does this mean for the hermeneutics task when interpreting the Bible?

Long

1. Explain the difference between *exegesis* and *hermeneutics*, outlining the components of each of these vital interpretive tasks.

Quiz

1. The aim of good interpretation is simple:
    a) To get at the "unique meaning of the text"
    b) To get at the "relevant meaning of the text"
    c) To get at the "plain meaning of the text"
    d) To get at the "popular meaning of the text"

2. If the plain meaning is what interpretation is all about, then why interpret? Why not just read? Does not the plain meaning come simply from reading? Such arguments are both naive and unrealistic because of:
    a) The nature of the reader
    b) The nature of Scripture
    c) The nature of relevancy
    d) A & B
    e) B & C

3. Because the Bible is God's message, it has eternal relevance; it speaks to all humankind, in every age and in every culture. But because God chose to speak his word through human words in history, every book in the Bible also has historical particularity; each document is conditioned by:
    a) The language, time, and culture in which it was originally written

b) The language, time, and culture in which it is interpreted

c) The language, time, and culture in which it is read

d) The language, time, and culture in which it was discovered

4. The task of interpreting involves two levels:

a) Eisegesis and hermeneutics

b) Exegesis and hermeneutics

c) Exegesis and homiletics

d) Eisegesis and homiletics

5. Exegesis involves the careful, systematic study of the Scripture to discover:

a) The relevant, cultural meaning

b) The original, possible meaning

c) The here-and-now meaning

d) The original, intended meaning

6. The expressions "what Jesus *meant* by that was . . ." and "back in those days, they used to . . ." are examples of what kinds of expressions?

a) Hermeneutical expressions

b) Eisegetical expressions

c) Exegetical expressions

d) Homiletical expressions

7. What is the most important contextual question you will ever ask?

a) What's the point?

b) What's my point?

c) What's it mean?

d) What's its relevance?

8. Questions of "content" have to do with:

a) The meanings of words

b) Words' grammatical relationships in sentences

c) The choice of the original text where the manuscripts differ from one another

d) Items of historical context

e) All of the above

9. What are three important tools for doing good exegesis?
   a) An original language translation, a good Bible dictionary, good commentaries
   b) A good translation, a good Bible dictionary, good commentaries
   c) A good translation, a good cultural dictionary, good commentaries
   d) A good translation, a good Bible dictionary, good sermon illustrations

10. Hermeneutics asks questions about the Bible's meaning in:
    a) The "here and now"
    b) The "there and then"
    c) The "original and purpose"
    d) The "history and context"

CHAPTER 2

The Basic Tool: A Good Translation

You Should Know

- Differences that exist between the original language and the receptor language in matters of words and grammar; differences that exist between the original language and the receptor language in idioms; differences that exist between the original language and the receptor language in matters of culture; differences that exist between the original language and the receptor language in matters of history

- Theory of translation is the degree to which one is willing to go in order to bridge the gap between the original and receptor languages, either in use of words and grammar or in bridging the historical distance by offering a modern equivalent.

- Original Bible languages: Hebrew, Aramaic, Greek

- Textual criticism: the science that attempts to discover the original texts of ancient documents

- External evidence: the quality and age of the manuscripts that support a given variant

- Internal evidence: the scribal habits and tendencies of copyists and authors analyzed by scholars that account for variants

- Original language: the language that one is translating *from*

- Receptor language: the language that one is translating *into*

- Formal equivalence: the attempt to keep as close to the "form" of the Hebrew or Greek, both words and grammar, as can be conveniently put into understandable English

- Functional equivalence: the attempt to keep the meaning of the Hebrew or Greek but to put their words and idioms into what would be the normal way of saying the same thing in English

Essay Questions

Short

1. What is textual criticism, and what evidence does it consider? Give some examples of such evidence. Why isn't textual criticism an exact science?

2. What does "theory of translation" mean? Explain what this unit suggests is the "best" theory of translation.

3. Explain the differences between formal equivalence and functional equivalence approaches to grammar and syntax, and why translation by functional equivalence is to be preferred.

Long

1. The way various translations handle the problem of "historical distance" often results in several kinds of problems. Briefly summarize each of the six kinds of problem and offer an example of each.

Quiz

1. The sixty-six books of the Protestant Bible were originally written in what languages?

   a) Hebrew and Greek
   b) Hebrew, Aramaic, and Greek
   c) Hebrew, Greek, and Syriac
   d) Greek only

2. What two choices do translators make when translating the Scriptures from the original language into English?

   a) Textual and hermeneutical
   b) Textual and cultural

   c) Textual and linguistic
   d) Hermeneutical and linguistic

3. Textual criticism is a science that works with careful controls that depend on what evidence?

   a) External evidence
   b) Cultural evidence
   c) Internal evidence
   d) Relevant evidence
   e) A and C

4. When translators are faced with a choice between two or more variants resulting from internal evidence of copyists and authors:

   a) Translators usually can detect which readings are the mistakes through relying on the Holy Spirit.
   b) Translators usually do not have enough evidence to make such decisions.
   c) Translators usually can detect which readings are the mistakes because of scholarly analysis of scribal habits and tendencies.
   d) Translators usually have to rely on their gut instinct or the democratic voting process of a translation committee.

5. When sifting through the internal evidence of the Bible, what kind of choices do translators have to make?

   a) Textual choices
   b) Application choices
   c) Hermeneutical choices
   d) Homiletical choices

6. Which translation philosophy attempts to keep as close to the form of the Hebrew or Greek, both words and grammar, as can be conveniently put into understandable English?

   a) Formal equivalence
   b) Functional equivalence
   c) Free translation
   d) All translating philosophies

7. Which translation philosophy attempts to keep the meaning of the Hebrew or Greek but to put their words and idioms into what would be the normal way of saying the same thing in English?

 a) Formal equivalence
 b) Functional equivalence
 c) Free translation
 d) All translating philosophies

8. When it comes to the best theory of translation, when something has to "give" in trying to remain faithful to both the original languages and the receptor language, it should be in favor of:

 a) The original language
 b) The receptor language
 c) Neither should "give"
 d) Both should "give"

9. When it comes to euphemisms, a translator has three choices. Which is probably the best?

 a) Translate literally but perhaps leave an English-speaking reader bewildered or guessing.
 b) Translate the formal equivalent but perhaps offend or shock the reader.
 c) Translate with a functionally equivalent euphemism.
 d) All of the above

10. The KJV's repeated "and it came to pass," in which the Hebrew narrative verb form that lies behind it is translated literally and woodenly, is an example of which problem of historical distance?

 a) Euphemism
 b) Vocabulary
 c) Wordplay
 d) Grammar and syntax

ANSWER KEY

1. B, 2. C, 3. E, 4. C, 5. A, 6. A, 7. B, 8. B, 9. C, 10. D

CHAPTER 3

The Epistles: Learning to Think Contextually

You Should Know

- Adolf Deissmann made a distinction between letters and epistles.
- Think paragraphs in order to trace epistle arguments.
- Epistles: an artistic literary form intended for the public
- New Testament real letters: Paul's Epistles, 2 John, 3 John
- Form of ancient letters: name of the writer; name of the recipient; greeting; prayer wish or thanksgiving; body; final greeting and farewell
- Occasional documents: documents arising out of a specific occasion; documents intended for a specific occasion
- Task theology: theology being written for or brought to bear on the task at hand
- Kinds of historical context notes: recipient characteristics, author's attitude, specific occasion, letter's divisions
- Epistle content question: What is the author saying; why did the author say it?

Essay Questions

Short

1. What does it mean that the New Testament epistles are "occasional documents?" The occasional nature of the epistles means that they are

not first of all theological treatises. What does this mean? Why is this significant to interpreting the epistles?

2. What are the four kinds of notes one should make when reading through a New Testament epistle? Explain why each kind of observation might be important.

3. Why is it important to learn to think in paragraphs? What does this accomplish?

Long

1. Summarize and explain how the major non-Gospel New Testament books mirror or do not mirror the formal elements of ancient letters.

Quiz

1. Who was it who made a distinction between letters and epistles on the basis of the vast papyrus discoveries?
   a) Rudolf Bultmann
   b) Adolf Deissmann
   c) Karl Barth
   d) Peter Stuhlmacher

2. What standard form do ancient letters take, which the New Testament forms mirror?
   a) Name of the recipient; name of the writer; greeting; prayer wish or thanksgiving; body; final greeting and farewell
   b) Name of the writer; name of the recipient; greeting; body; prayer wish or thanksgiving; final greeting and farewell
   c) Name of the writer; name of the recipient; greeting; prayer wish or thanksgiving; body; final greeting and farewell
   d) Greeting; name of the writer; name of the recipient; prayer wish or thanksgiving; body; final greeting and farewell

3. There is one item that all of the Epistles have in common, and this is the crucial item to note in reading and interpreting them: They are all what are technically called

a) Rhetorical documents
b) Occasional documents
c) Spiritual documents
d) Ecclesial documents

4. What is the first thing one must try to do with any of the Epistles when interpreting them?

a) Understand the historical context and situation to which the author was speaking.
b) Understand the contemporary application the author was conveying.
c) Understand the theology the author was outlining.
d) Understand the argument, paragraph by paragraph.

5. When forming a tentative but informed reconstruction of the situation to which the author is speaking, what do you do?

a) Consult a Bible dictionary or the introduction to a commentary.
b) Read the whole letter in one sitting.
c) Trace the argument, paragraph by paragraph.
d) All of the above
e) A & B

6. After establishing the historical context, what is the next thing you must do with any of the Epistles when interpreting them?

a) Understand the historical context and situation to which the author was speaking.
b) Understand the contemporary application the author was conveying.
c) Understand the theology the author was outlining.
d) Understand the argument the author was presenting, paragraph by paragraph.

7. When tracing the argument in a New Testament epistle you should be able to state what two aspects of the content?

a) What the author is saying; where the author said it
b) What the author is saying; why the author said it
c) What the author is saying; how the author said it
d) What the author is saying; when the author said it

8. When successfully summarizing the point of the New Testament author in an epistle:

a) The exegesis is self-contained.
b) There is nothing in the paragraph that does not fit into the argument.
c) The analysis makes perfectly good sense of everything.
d) All of the above

9. In many cases the reason the problem passages are so difficult for us is that, frankly:

a) They were not written to us.
b) They were written to us, so the message hits close to home.
c) We don't have enough historical context.
d) The literary context is difficult to grasp.

10. Despite some uncertainty as to some of the precise details of problem passages, one needs to discern:

a) What cannot be said for certain about a given passage and what is merely possible but not certain
b) What can be said for certain about a given passage and what is probable
c) What can be said for certain about a given passage and what is merely possible but not certain
d) None of the above

CHAPTER 4

The Epistles: The Hermeneutical Question

You Should Know

- Whether it is legitimate to extend the application of a passage to other contexts, or to make a first-century case-specific matter apply to a context totally foreign to its first-century setting; whether God's word to us in texts where there are comparable situations and comparable particulars should be limited to its original intent

- When passages speak to first-century issues that for the most part are without any twenty-first-century counterparts; when passages speak to problems that could happen also in the twenty-first century but are highly unlikely to do so; whether God's word to us in texts where there are comparable situations and comparable particulars should be limited to its original intent

- "Sometimes our theological problems with the Epistles derive from the fact that we are asking our questions of texts that by their occasional nature are answering their questions only."

- Problem of cultural relativity: what is cultural and belongs to the first century alone; what transcends culture and is a word for all seasons

- Commonsense hermeneutics: bringing our own form of common sense to the Bible; applying what we can from the Bible to our own situation

- The basic rule of hermeneutics: "A text cannot mean what it never could have meant to its author or readers."

- The second rule of hermeneutics: "Whenever we share comparable particulars with the first-century hearers, God's word to us is the same as his word to them."

- Matters of indifference: matters that tend to differ from culture to culture, even among genuine believers

- Problem of cultural relativity: the problem of God's eternal word having been given in historical particularity

- Problem of task theology: the problem of systematically presenting the theology that is either expressed in or derived from statements in the Epistles based on sound exegesis

Essay Questions

Short

1. Without necessarily intending to, we bring a number of things to the epistles as we read them. What are they, and how do they affect how we read the Bible? Provide an example for each.

2. Why can't a text mean what it never could have meant to its author or readers? How does this illustrate the principle that exegesis must always come first?

3. What is meant by the "second basic rule," a slightly different way of expressing our common hermeneutics?

Long

1. Explain how one can distinguish between items that are culturally relative on the one hand and those that transcend their original setting on the other hand, and are thus normative for all Christians of all times.

Quiz

1. What is the hermeneutical question?
   a) What do these texts mean to God?
   b) What do these texts mean to us?

    c) What do these texts mean to Paul?

    d) What do these texts mean to the original audience?

2. The big issue among Christians committed to Scripture as God's Word has to do with:

    a) Original intent

    b) Applicational relevancy

    c) Cultural relativity

    d) Divine inspiration

3. The great flaw with common hermeneutics is that we bring to the Epistles as we read them:

    a) Our theological heritage

    b) Our church traditions

    c) Our cultural norms

    d) Our existential concerns

    e) All of the above

4. A basic rule of hermeneutics is the premise that a text cannot mean what it never could have meant:

    a) To its author

    b) To its readers

    c) To us

    d) All of the above

    e) A & B

5. Whenever we share comparable particulars (i.e., similar specific life situations) with the first-century hearers:

    a) God's word to us is harder than his word to them.

    b) God's word to us is the same as his word to them.

    c) God's word to us is different than his word to them.

    d) God's word to us is easier than his word to them.

6. An extended application is usually seen to be legitimate because it is true, that is, it is clearly spelled out in other passages where that is the:

    a) Intent of the passage

    b) Implication of the passage

   c) Application of the passage

   d) None of the above

7. When the apostles' answers to non-contemporary problems speak to twenty-first-century Christians, proper hermeneutics should legitimately:

   a) Do exegesis with particular care so that we hear what God's word to them really was

   b) Apply the "principle" to genuinely comparable situations

   c) Allow the "principle" to become timeless, to be applied to any and every kind of situation

   d) A & B

8. When it comes to problems of particulars, the problem for us at a much later moment in history is how to distinguish:

   a) Matters of indifference from matters that don't count

   b) Matters of importance from matters that count

   c) Matters of indifference from matters that count

   d) Matters of urgency from matters that are ambiguous

9. What problem with respect to hermeneutics is the area where most present-day difficulties lie?

   a) The problem of extended application

   b) The problem of particulars

   c) The problem of cultural relativity

   d) The problem of task theology

10. One should be prepared to distinguish between what the New Testament itself sees as inherently moral and what is not. Importantly, Paul's sin lists never contain:

   a) Moral choices

   b) Cultural items

   c) Legal items

   d) Biblical choices

CHAPTER 5

The Old Testament Narratives: Their Proper Use

You Should Know

- Single most common type of biblical literature is narrative, which are purposeful stories retelling the historical events of the past that are intended to give meaning and direction for a given people in the present.

- Instead of concentrating on the clear meaning of the narrative, some relegate the text to merely reflecting another meaning beyond the text. This is known as allegorizing.

- Ignoring the full historical and literary contexts, and often the individual narrative, some people concentrate on small units only and thus miss interpretational clues, called decontextualizing.

- Basic narrative parts: characters, plot, plot resolution

- Metanarrative: the whole universal plan of God worked out through his creation and focusing primarily on God's chosen people

- Distinctive features of Hebrew narratives: narrator, scenes, characters, dialogue, plot, and structure

- Implicit teaching: narrative teaching that is clearly present in the story but not stated in so many words

- Moralizing: In asking "what is the moral of this story?", this approach involves the assumption that principles for living can be derived from all passages.

- Misappropriation: closely related to personalizing, it is to appropriate a narrative for purposes that are quite foreign to its reason for being there

Essay Questions

Short

1. All narratives, including biblical ones, have three basic parts: characters, plot, and plot resolution. Explain each component, particularly those of the biblical story.

2. Individual Old Testament narratives are not intended to teach moral lessons. Why not, and what do they teach instead?

3. How do people personalize and individualize readings of Scripture, and why is this an error of interpretation? Give an example or two.

Long

1. Old Testament biblical narratives are told on three levels. Summarize and explain each of those levels and how they function in the Bible.

Quiz

1. What type of events are recounted in biblical narratives and what is their intent?
    a) Moral events intended to give meaning and direction to people in the present
    b) Historical events intended to give meaning and direction to people in the present
    c) Allegorical events intended to give meaning and direction to people in the present
    d) Historical events intended to give meaning and direction to people in the past

2. Hebrew narratives have some distinctive features that include:
    a) Narrator, scenes, characters, dialogue, plot, and structure
    b) Narrator, scenes, characters, dialogue, plot, and moral lesson

    c) Narrator, scenes, characters, dialogue, plot, and allegory

    d) Narrator, audience, scenes, characters, dialogue, and plot

3. When it comes to Old Testament narratives, who is the one person not mentioned directly in the unfolding of the narrative?

    a) The protagonist

    b) The antagonist

    c) The narrator

    d) The hero

4. The predominant mode of narration in Hebrew narrative is built around:

    a) Characters

    b) Scenes

    c) Narrators

    d) Settings

5. What is the absolutely central element of Hebrew narratives?

    a) Characters

    b) Scenes

    c) Narrators

    d) Settings

6. Hebrew narrative uses a whole series of structural features to catch people's attention and keep them fastened on the narrative. We often overlook such features because these narratives were designed primarily for:

    a) Hearers, not readers

    b) Readers, not hearers

    c) Pastors, not students

    d) Students, not pastors

7. The book of Ruth has embedded within its narrative teaching that is clearly present in the story but not stated in so many words. This is called:

    a) Exegetical teaching

    b) Allegorical teaching

    c) Explicit teaching

    d) Implicit teaching

8. Instead of concentrating on the clear meaning of the narrative, some relegate the text to merely reflecting another meaning beyond the text. What common error of interpretation does this reflect?

   a) Allegorizing
   b) Moralizing
   c) Misappropriation
   d) Redefinition

9. When people "fleece" God as a way of finding God's will by adopting Gideon's narrative as their own, what error are they committing?

   a) Allegorizing
   b) Moralizing
   c) Misappropriation
   d) Redefinition

10. When the plain meaning of the text leaves people cold, producing no immediate spiritual delight, or says something other than what they wish it said, they are often tempted to engage in what error of interpretation? (p. 109)

   a) Allegorizing
   b) Moralizing
   c) Misappropriation
   d) Redefinition

CHAPTER 6

Acts: The Question of Historical Precedent

You Should Know

- Hellenistic historiography was written to encourage and/or entertain, as well as to inform, moralize, or offer an apologetic.

- The key to understanding the book of Acts is the Gentile mission.

- Luke's model in Acts is Gospel proclamation.

- Unless Scripture explicitly tells us we must do something, what is only narrated or described does not function in a normative way—unless it can be demonstrated on other grounds that the author intended it to function in this way.

- God's word is to be found in the intent of Scripture is a general maxim of hermeneutics for historical narratives in Acts.

- There is full justification for the later church's repeating of biblical patterns; but it is moot to argue that all Christians everywhere and always must repeat the pattern or they are disobedient to God's Word.

- Restoration mentality: looking back to the church and Christian experience in the first century as the norm to be restored; looking back to the church and Christian experience in the first century as the ideal to be approximated

- Hellenistic historiography: a kind of history writing that had its roots in Thucydides and flourished during the Hellenistic period

- Key divisions of Acts: 1:1–6:7; 6:8–9:31; 9:32–12:24; 12:25–16:5; 16:6–19:20; 19:21–28:30

- Categories of Christian doctrinal statements derived from Scripture: theology, ethics, experience, practice

Essay Questions

Short

1. How are our readings of Old Testament narratives and the book of Acts related?

2. Explain why it is important that Luke, the author of Acts, was a Gentile, whose inspired narrative is at the same time an excellent example of Hellenistic historiography.

3. What are the principles with regard to the hermeneutics of historical narrative in the book of Acts?

Long

1. The book of Acts can be seen to be composed of six sections. After reading through the book of Acts in one sitting, summarize each section and explain how each section contributes to the overall "movement" of the book, as well as the key to each new forward thrust.

Quiz

1. Why do most people come to the book of Acts?
   a) They are greatly interested in historical details about the history of the primitive church.
   b) They have apologetic interests, proving the Bible to be true by showing Luke's accuracy as a historian.
   c) They come to the book for purely religious or devotional reasons.
   d) They want to know what the early Christians were like so that they may inspire us or serve as models.
   e) C & D

2. What kind of history do Luke's two volumes (Luke and Acts) reflect?
   a) Hebrew historiography
   b) Gallic historiography

c) Hellenistic historiography

d) Roman historiography

3. Exegesis of Acts includes not only the purely historical questions like what happened but also:

a) Homiletical ones

b) Theological ones

c) Philosophical ones

d) Applicational ones

4. Throughout the book of Acts, who plays the absolutely leading role at every key juncture?

a) Peter

b) John Mark

c) Paul

d) The Holy Spirit

5. One will surely miss the point of the book of Acts on the basis of its structure and content alone without any statement of purpose that does not include:

a) The Gentile mission

b) The Jewish mission

c) Paul's mission

d) The Roman mission

6. Much of Acts is intended by Luke to serve as a model. What is this model?

a) Church polity

b) Church practices

c) Gospel proclamation

d) Gospel theology

7. When it comes to the hermeneutics of Acts, what question should concern us? (p. 123–124)

a) How do the individual doctrines in Acts function as precedents for the later church, or do they?

b) How do the individual practices in Acts function as precedents for the later church, or do they?

c) How do the individual narratives in Acts function as precedents for the early church, or do they?

d) How do the individual narratives in Acts function as precedents for the later church, or do they?

8. In general, doctrinal statements derived from Scripture fall into categories and levels. Almost everything Christians derive from Scripture by way of precedent is in which category? (p. 125)

a) The category of Christian theology, and always at the first level

b) The category of Christian experience or practice, and always at the secondary level

c) The category of Christian ethics, and always at the secondary level

d) The category of Christian experience or practice, and always at the first level

9. As a general maxim of hermeneutics, especially when it comes to the historical narratives in Acts, God's word is to be found in the:

a) Application of Scripture

b) Culture of Scripture

c) Intent of Scripture

d) Implication of Scripture

10. The decision as to whether certain practices or patterns from the book of Acts are repeatable should be guided by the following consideration(s): (p. 130–131)

a) Strong cases can be made only when one pattern is found and repeated within the New Testament itself.

b) When patterns are ambiguous or occur once, later Christians should repeat them only if they are divinely ordained or in harmony with what is taught elsewhere in Scripture.

c) What is culturally conditioned is either not repeatable at all or must be translated into the new or differing culture.

d) All of the above

CHAPTER 7

The Gospels: One Story, Many Dimensions

You Should Know

- Requirements for exegesis of the four Gospels include the historical setting of Jesus and the historical setting of the authors of the Gospels.

- Historical context of the Gospels includes the religion and culture of first-century Palestine, the individual authors' lives and context, and the reason the authors wrote and the situation they were addressing.

- "One dare not think they can properly interpret the Gospels without a clear understanding of the concept of the kingdom of God in the ministry of Jesus."

- The kingdom of God is the time of God's rule; the new, messianic age; and considered to be already, not yet.

- Forms of Jesus' teachings: parables, hyperbole, proverbs, poetry, and questions

- Literary context of the Gospels is the place in the Gospels where the evangelists chose to put the deeds and teaching of Jesus.

- Think horizontally: When studying a pericope in any one gospel, it is usually helpful to be aware of the parallels in the other gospels.

- Think vertically: When reading or studying a narrative or teaching in the Gospels, one should try to be aware of the historical contexts of both Jesus and the evangelist.

- Three principles of gospel composition: selectivity, arrangement, and adaptation

Essay Questions

Short

1. What is the literary context of the Gospels and Jesus's deeds and teachings? Why is it important that when reading or studying a narrative or teaching in the Gospels, one should try to be aware of the historical contexts of both Jesus and the evangelist?

2. Three principles were at work in the composition of the Gospels: selectivity, arrangement, and adaptation. Briefly summarize each of these principles.

3. In what way should the teachings and imperatives of Jesus in the Gospels be brought into the twenty-first century in the same way as we do with Paul and the epistles?

Long

1. What is the kingdom of God? Explain how this important concept fits with the New Testament eschatological view.

Quiz

1. The content of the Gospels can be divided roughly into:
    a) The sayings and actions
    b) The actions and teachings
    c) The sayings and narratives
    d) The actions and narratives

2. Exegesis of the four Gospels requires us to think in terms of:
    a) The historical setting of Jesus
    b) The historical setting of the authors
    c) The historical setting of the current audience
    d) The historical setting of the Old Testament
    e) A & B

3. What form(s) did the teachings of Jesus take?
    a) Parables
    b) Hyperbole

    c) Proverbs

    d) Poetry

    e) Questions

    f) All of the above

4. Which gospel is especially interested in explaining the nature of Jesus's messiahship in light of Isaiah's "second exodus" motif?

    a) Matthew

    b) Mark

    c) Luke

    d) John

5. When interpreting or reading one of the Gospels, one needs to keep in mind: (p. 140)

    a) There are four of them.

    b) They were written by Jesus himself.

    c) They are "two-level" documents.

    d) A & C

6. The best explanation of all the data regarding verbal similarity among the Gospels is that one writer wrote his gospel first, probably in part at least from his recollection of Peter's preaching and teaching. Which one?

    a) Matthew

    b) Mark

    c) Luke

    d) John

7. For the most part, the hermeneutical principles for the Gospels are a combination of what has been said about which other genres?

    a) The Epistles and historical narratives

    b) The law(s) and historical narratives

    c) The Epistles and prophetic books

    d) The wisdom literature and law(s)

8. The miracle stories are recorded:

    a) To offer morals in how to live in the kingdom of God

    b) To serve as precedents for our own day-to-day lives and ministries

c) To illustrate the power of the kingdom breaking in through Jesus's ministry

d) All of the above

9. One dare not think they can properly interpret the Gospels without a clear understanding of which important aspect of Jesus's ministry?

a) The miracles

b) The Sermon on the Mount

c) The kingdom of God

d) The parables

10. The hermeneutical key to much of the New Testament, and especially the ministry and teaching of Jesus, is to be found in what tension with the kingdom of God?

a) It is progressive and conservative.

b) It is already and not yet.

c) It is rapturing and escaping.

d) All of the above

CHAPTER 8

The Parables: Do You Get the Point?

You Should Know

- "The secret of the kingdom of God has been given to you. But to those on the outside everything is said in parables so that, 'they may be ever seeing but never perceiving, and ever hearing but never understanding; otherwise they might turn and be forgiven!'" (Mark 4:11–12)

- When interpreting contextless parables, determine the points of reference and determine the original audience.

- The parables of the kingdom express the dawning of the time of salvation with the coming of Jesus.

- The hermeneutical task of parables is to translate the parable's point into our own context and immerse yourself in the meaning of the kingdom in Jesus's ministry.

- An example of a true parable: the Good Samaritan

- An example of a similitude: the yeast and the dough

- An example of a metaphor and simile: "You are the salt of the earth"

- The function of parables calls for a response.

- Points of reference: The parts of the story that draw the hearer into it and the parts of the story with which one is to identify in some way as the story proceeds

- Intended response: The parts of the story where the point of the parable is found

Essay Questions

Short

1. How have Christians interpreted the parables allegorically? Why does this course insist they are not allegories?

2. Briefly explain a *true parable*, a *similitude*, and *metaphors* and *similes*. Identify an example of each and explain why it illustrates this kind of parable.

3. The best clues as to what the parables are is to be found in their function. How do these stories function in the life and ministry of Jesus?

Long

1. The task of interpretation with parables is a combination of three things: (1) sit and listen to the parable, (2) identify the points of reference intended by Jesus, and (3) try to determine how the original hearers would have identified with the story, and heard it. Using these elements, interpret the Good Samaritan parable in Luke 10:25–37.

Quiz

1. The reason for the long history of the misinterpretation of the parables can be traced back to something Jesus himself said in which gospel passage?
   a) Mark 1:15
   b) Mark 4:10–12
   c) Matthew 5–7
   d) Luke 4:18–19

2. If we have trouble at times understanding the parables, it is because:
   a) They are allegories for which we need some special interpretive key.
   b) They require discovering the original audience.
   c) They are beyond our understanding.
   d) They require the Holy Spirit.

3. The best clues as to what the parables are is to be found in their:
    a) Interpretation
    b) Application
    c) Form
    d) Function

4. The point of the parable story is to be found in the:
    a) Intended response
    b) Allegorical reading
    c) Cultural milieu
    d) Contemporary application

5. When it comes to the task of interpretation of a parable, what is needed?
    a) Sit and listen to the parable again and again.
    b) Identify the points of reference intended by Jesus that would have been picked up by the original hearers.
    c) Try to determine how the original hearers would have identified with the story, and therefore what they would have heard.
    d) All of the above

6. The key to understanding the parables is determining:
    a) The allegory
    b) The points of reference
    c) Unexpected turns
    d) The original audience
    e) B & D

7. When it comes to interpreting parables found in the Gospels without their original historical context, it is a matter of: (p. 162)
    a) Trying to determine the points of reference
    b) Trying to determine the original audience
    c) Trying to determine the cultural milieu
    d) Trying to determine the contemporary application
    e) A & B

8. What do the parables of the kingdom express?
    a) The dawning of the time of salvation with the coming of Jesus
    b) The dawning of the time of progress with the coming of Jesus

c) The dawning of the time of progress with the teaching of Jesus

d) The dawning of the time of salvation with the coming of the church

9. Jesus's kingdom parables are not to be allegorized, but rather are to be heard as:

a) Calls to wait for Jesus to return

b) Calls to apply the law of God to the nations of man

c) Calls to respond to Jesus and his mission

d) Calls to build a progressive social movement

10. Through the exegetical process we can discover the meaning of parables, their point, with a high degree of accuracy, because they are in:

a) An oral context

b) A written context

c) A cultural context

d) An applicational context

CHAPTER 9

The Law(s): Covenant Stipulations for Israel

You Should Know

- Exodus 20 is the beginning of the law in the Old Testament.

- A *suzerain covenant* is a binding contract made between an all-powerful overlord and a weaker, dependent vassal; a relationship that guaranteed benefits and protection from an overlord to a vassal; a relationship that obligated sole loyalty from a vassal to an overlord; and an agreement requiring vassals to keep rules of behavior and warning of punishment from an overlord for disloyalty.

- When its own purposes are properly understood, the law should be recognized as beneficial to the Israelites, a marvelous example of God's mercy and grace to his people.

- Civil laws include laws that specify penalties for various crimes (major and minor) for which one might be arrested and tried in Israel.

- Ritual laws are those that told the people of Israel how to carry out the practices of old-covenant worship.

- Ethical laws are laws that serve to support the two basic laws on which depend all the Law and the Prophets: "Love the Lord your God with all your heart and with all your soul and with all your mind" and "Love your neighbor as yourself."

- Six parts of a covenant: preamble, prologue, stipulations, witnesses, sanctions, and document clause

- Law's role in the life of Israel set out parameters of relationships and established loyalty between God and his people.

- Apodictic laws: commands that begin with "do" or "do not," telling the Israelites the sorts of things they are supposed to do to fulfill their part of the covenant with God

- Casuistic laws: the commands that are case-by-case laws involving third-person descriptions, giving examples of what may be the case or what may happen, and what ought to be done if it does

Essay Questions

Short

1. What is a covenant, and after what kind of covenant was Israel's with God modeled? Summarize the six parts of the covenant between God and Israel.

2. Even though the Old Testament laws are not our laws, why would it be a mistake to conclude that the law is no longer a valuable part of the Bible?

3. In what way was the law beneficial to the Israelites? How did the laws about food, shedding blood, and other unusual laws benefit them?

Long

1. This unit outlines a number of dos-and-don'ts principles to help you avoid mistaken applications of the law while seeing its instructive and faith-building character. Summarize and explain the twelve principles given in this session.

Quiz

1. The role(s) the law played in Israel's history was as:
    a) A gift
    b) A boundary

c) A code of conduct

d) A means of salvation

e) A & B

2. What connotation(s) does the word "law" have in the Old Testament?

a) The individual 600-plus specific commandments given to the Israelites

b) All of the laws collectively given to Israel to keep as evidence of their loyalty to God

c) The Pentateuch (Genesis to Deuteronomy)

d) The New Testament's reference theologically to the entire Old Testament religious system

e) The New Testament reference to the Old Testament law as it was interpreted by the rabbis

f) All of the above

3. What question(s) is the most difficult problem for most Christians with regard to the Old Testament commandments?

a) Do any of these specific legal formulations apply to us?

b) How do any of these specific legal formulations apply to us?

c) How did the specific legal formulations apply to Israel?

d) Why do these specific legal formulations still apply to us?

e) A & B

4. Which well-known covenant format did God use when he constituted the binding contract between himself and his vassal, Israel?

a) Sinai covenant

b) Suzerain covenant

c) Babylonian covenant

d) Akkadian covenant

5. The covenant format had six parts to it, including and in this order:

a) Prologue, preamble, stipulations, witnesses, sanctions, and document clause

b) Preamble, prologue, sanctions, witnesses, stipulations, and document clause

    c) Preamble, prologue, stipulations, witnesses, sanctions, and document clause

    d) Preamble, prologue, stipulations, witnesses, blessings, and document clause

6. Part of the old covenant is renewed in the new covenant. Which parts are actually restated in the New Testament as applicable to Christians?

    a) Ritual law

    b) Ethical law

    c) Civic law

    d) Food law

    e) B & D

7. What role did the law play in the life of Israel? How did it function?

    a) It was thought of in Israel as a "means of salvation."

    b) It set out parameters of relationships and established loyalty between God and his people.

    c) It represented the terms of the agreement of loyalty that Israel had with God.

    d) B & C

8. What laws are "do" and "do not" laws that told the Israelites the sorts of things they were supposed to do to fulfill their part of the covenant with God?

    a) Apodictic laws

    b) Food laws

    c) Casuistic laws

    d) Ritualistic laws

9. What laws are case-by-case conditional laws that describe certain conditions that may prevail in certain types of situations involving certain types of people, but not necessarily in every situation involving every person?

    a) Apodictic laws

    b) Food laws

    c) Casuistic laws

    d) Ritualistic laws

10. Ethically, how do the Old Testament laws compare to other ancient law codes?

- a) The Old Testament law represents some progress over such codes.
- b) The Old Testament law represents a regression compared with such codes.
- c) The Old Testament law represents a quantum leap ahead over such codes.
- d) The Old Testament law is comparable to such codes.

CHAPTER 10

The Prophets: Enforcing the Covenant in Israel

You Should Know

- In the Prophetic Books we hear from God via the prophets and very little about the prophets themselves.

- The function of the prophet in Israel included being a covenant enforcement mediator, bearing God's message, acting as God's direct representative, and bearing an unoriginal message.

- The lawsuit prophetic utterance is a prophetic literary form that imaginatively portrays God as the plaintiff, prosecuting attorney, judge, and bailiff in a court case against the defendant, Israel.

- The woe prophetic utterance is a prophetic literary form in which God makes predictions of imminent doom containing, either explicitly or implicitly, three elements that uniquely characterize this form: an announcement of distress, the reason for the distress, and a prediction of doom.

- The promise prophetic utterance is a prophetic literary form, also known as a "salvation oracle," containing these elements: reference to the future, mention of radical change, and mention of blessing.

- The enactment prophetic utterance is a prophetic literary form in which God sometimes told prophets not merely to speak his word but also to accompany that word with symbolic actions that would vividly reinforce the concepts contained in what the prophets spoke.

- The messenger speech prophetic utterance is a form of prophetic utterance, often occurring alongside of, or as part of, one of the others using such phrases as "this is what the Lord says . . ."

- Major Prophets: Isaiah, Jeremiah, Ezekiel, and Daniel

- Minor Prophets: the final twelve books of the Old Testament

- Sensus plenior: the secondary meaning of an Old Testament passage that is offered in the New Testament and a function of inspiration

Essay Questions

Short

1. Describe and explain the simple pattern of the prophetic books.

2. Why do you need to understand both the large and specific historical contexts for all the prophetic books in order to do good exegesis?

3. What is *sensus plenior*? How does it relate to prophecy, as well as to the New Testament?

Long

1. To understand what God would say to us through the prophets, we must first have a clear understanding as to the role and function of the prophet in Israel. Summarize and explain the function of the prophet in Israel.

Quiz

1. The Prophetic Books are among the most difficult parts of the Bible for people of later times to interpret or read with understanding. The reasons for this are primarily related to misunderstandings as to their:

    a) Purpose and meaning
    b) Function and form
    c) Context and history
    d) All of the above

2. We have great trouble putting the words spoken by the prophets in their original historical context, and it is often hard for us to see what they are referring to and why, because we are far removed from:

    a) The religious life of ancient Israel

    b) The historical life of ancient Israel

    c) The cultural life of ancient Israel

    d) All of the above

3. What Old Testament figure is a paradigm or model for the mediating role of the prophets?

    a) Abraham

    b) Moses

    c) David

    d) Elijah

4. Whose message did the prophets bear?

    a) Their own

    b) God's

    c) The king's

    d) Israel's

5. The prophets were inspired by God to present to their generation the essential content of what original message?

    a) The Abrahamic covenant's blessings and curses

    b) The Davidic covenant's eternal kingdom

    c) The Mosaic covenant's warnings and promises

    d) The exilic trials and tribulations

6. In what books did God express to his people the original Mosaic covenant's warnings and promises?

    a) Exodus, Leviticus, Numbers, and Deuteronomy

    b) Genesis, Exodus, Leviticus, and Numbers

    c) 1 Samuel, 1 Kings, and 1 Chronicles

    d) Proverbs, Psalms, and Ecclesiastes

7. When one comes to the actual study or exegetically informed reading of the Prophetic Books, the first thing one must learn to do is:

a) Think paragraphs
b) Think sentences
c) Think pericopes
d) Think oracles

8. Which form of prophetic utterance imaginatively portrays God as the plaintiff, prosecuting attorney, judge, and bailiff in a court case against the defendant, Israel?

a) The lawsuit
b) The woe
c) The promise
d) The enactment prophecy
e) The messenger speech

9. In which form of prophetic utterance did God sometimes tell prophets not merely to speak his word but also to accompany that word with symbolic actions that would vividly reinforce the concepts contained in what the prophets spoke?

a) The lawsuit
b) The woe
c) The promise
d) The enactment prophecy
e) The messenger speech

10. Which form of prophetic utterance is the most common, often occurring alongside of, or as part of, one of the others using such phrases as "this is what the Lord says . . ."?

a) The lawsuit
b) The woe
c) The promise
d) The enactment prophecy
e) The messenger speech

CHAPTER 11

The Psalms: Israel's Prayers and Ours

You Should Know

- Laments are psalms that help individuals or the corporate body express struggles, suffering, or disappointment to the Lord.

- Thanksgiving psalms are used to express joy to the Lord because something had gone well, because circumstances were good, or because people had reason to render thanks to God for his faithfulness, protection, and benefits.

- Hymns of praise center on the praise of God for who God is, for God's greatness and beneficence toward the whole earth as well as God's own people.

- Salvation-history psalms focus on reviewing the history of God's saving works among the people of Israel, especially his deliverance of them from bondage in Egypt and his creation of them as a people.

- Psalms of celebration and affirmation include several kinds of psalms, including covenant renewal liturgies; royal psalms dealing with the kingship; psalms celebrating the enthronement of the king; and Songs of Zion celebrating Jerusalem.

- Wisdom psalms are psalms praising the merits of wisdom and the wise life that may be read profitably along with the book of Proverbs.

- Songs of trust center their attention on the fact that, even in times of despair, God's goodness and care for his people ought to be expressed.

- Imprecatory psalms help guide and channel our anger to and through God by verbalizing to him such emotions we have toward others.

- Hebrew poetry, by its very nature, was addressed to the mind through the heart.

- Benefits of psalms: serve as a guide to worship; demonstrate how we can relate honestly to God; demonstrate the importance of reflection and meditation on what God has done for us

Essay Questions

Short

1. As beloved as they are, why do the psalms present a special difficulty for understanding? What reality about Psalms presents us with a unique problem of hermeneutics in Scripture?

2. How did the psalms function within the life of Israel? How do the words in Psalms spoken to God function for us as a word from God today?

3. The authors caution that "the psalms do not guarantee a pleasant life." Explain what they mean and why this is important to the hermeneutical task of interpreting the psalms.

Long

1. As musical poems, psalms are also a form of literature with certain distinct literary features. Summarize and explain these features.

Quiz

1. The psalms are beneficial and profitable to us when used for the purposes intended by God, because they:
   a) Teach us moral lessons
   b) Help us express ourselves

   c) Instruct us in doctrine
   d) Offer prophetic insights into God's plans

2. Hebrew poetry, by its very nature, was addressed to:

   a) The heart through the mind
   b) The mind through the heart
   c) The intellect through narratives
   d) The emotions through narratives

3. One of the most important items to remember in reading or interpreting psalms is that they are:

   a) Musical narratives
   b) Musical prophecies
   c) Musical prayers
   d) Musical poems

4. Because the vocabulary of poetry is purposefully metaphorical, one must take care to look for:

   a) The intent of the metaphor
   b) The allegory of the metaphor
   c) The hidden meaning of the metaphor
   d) Ways to press the metaphor

5. When reading the psalms, readers should regularly ask themselves:

   a) What is the *historical narrative* behind the psalm I am reading?
   b) What *type* of psalm am I reading?
   c) Which *author* wrote the psalm I am reading?
   d) What is the *era* of the psalm I am reading?

6. Which psalms constitute the largest group, helping individuals or the corporate body express struggles, suffering, or disappointment to the Lord?

   a) Lament
   b) Thanksgiving
   c) Salvation-history
   d) Celebration and affirmation
   e) Songs of trust

7. Which psalms were used to express joy to the Lord because something had gone well, because circumstances were good, or because people had reason to render thanks to God for his faithfulness, protection, and benefits?

    a) Lament
    b) Thanksgiving
    c) Salvation-history
    d) Celebration and affirmation
    e) Wisdom

8. Which psalms center their attention on the fact that, even in times of despair, God's goodness and care for his people ought to be expressed?

    a) Lament
    b) Thanksgiving
    c) Salvation-history
    d) Celebration and affirmation
    e) Songs of trust

9. Lament psalms carry these elements, in this order:

    a) Address, complaint, trust, deliverance, assurance, and praise
    b) Address, complaint, appeal, deliverance, assurance, and testimony
    c) Introduction, distress, appeal, deliverance, and testimony
    d) Introduction, complaint, distress, appeal, deliverance, assurance, and testimony

10. Imprecatory psalms help guide and channel our anger to and through:

    a) Our enemies
    b) Our friends
    c) God
    d) The Bible

ANSWER KEY

1. B, 2. B, 3. D, 4. A, 5. B, 6. A, 7. B, 8. E, 9. A, 10. C

CHAPTER 12

Wisdom: Then and Now

You Should Know

- Biblical wisdom is the ability to make godly choices in life.

- The focus of wisdom literature is people and their behavior.

- Wisdom in Job offers wisdom through a story about God's gracious superintendence of suffering and the way that innocent suffering can truly glorify God. This wisdom is offered through a carefully structured dialogue with the goal of establishing that what happens in life does not always happen either because God desires it or because it is fair.

- Wisdom in Ecclesiastes presents wisdom through a monologue coming to terms with the very important word *hebel*—"Vanity" or "meaningless."

- Wisdom in Song of Songs comes through a lengthy love song, a ballad about human romance, written in the style of ancient Near Eastern lyric poetry, dealing explicitly with the "wise choice" of marital and sexual fidelity.

- Wisdom books: Proverbs, Job, Ecclesiastes, and Song of Songs

- Prudential wisdom: the memorable aphorisms people can use to help themselves make responsible choices in life

- Speculative wisdom: the wisdom concentrating on wrestling with the great issues of life, expressing and reminding the reader of the hard questions

- Wisdom in Proverbs concentrates mostly on practical attitudes and behavior in everyday life; teaches old-fashioned, basic values; and presents a sharp contrast between choosing a life of wisdom and a life of folly.

- A proverb: points toward truth, is a brief expression of a truth, and is a particular expression of a truth

Essay Questions

Short

1. Summarize some rules that will help you make proper use of the book of Proverbs and be true to their divinely inspired intent.

2. When it comes to the book of Job, what do you need to keep in mind when reading the dialogue? What is its very important goal? How do the dialogue and the storyline combine to produce the Old Testament's paramount exemplar of speculative wisdom?

3. Song of Songs deals explicitly with a category of wisdom found in Proverbs: the "wise choice" of marital and sexual fidelity. Why do you think we need an entire book on this topic in the Bible? How does the book center on and express human love?

Long

1. Biblically speaking, what is wisdom? Traditionally, the wisdom books have been misused in three ways. Summarize and explain each of those ways.

Quiz

1. Biblical wisdom is the:
    a) Ability to make wise choices in life
    b) Ability to make correct choices in life
    c) Ability to make godly choices in life
    d) Ability to make profitable choices in life

2. Non-Israelite wisdom also had as its goal the making of the best choices, the purpose being to achieve the best life. What the inspired biblical wisdom added to this was the crucial idea that:
    a) The only good choices are godly choices.
    b) The only good choices are wise choices.

c) The only good choices are correct choices.

d) The only good choices are profitable choices.

3. Wisdom literature tends to focus on people and their:

a) Beliefs

b) Perspectives

c) Mindset

d) Behavior

4. Memorable aphorisms people can use to help themselves make responsible choices in life are known as:

a) Speculative wisdom

b) Prudential wisdom

c) Old-fashioned wisdom

d) Religious wisdom

5. A proverb:

a) Does not state everything about a truth

b) Points toward truth

c) Is a brief expression of a truth

d) Is a particular expression of a truth

e) All of the above

6. The goal of the dialogue in the book of Job is to establish convincingly in the mind of the reader that what happens in life:

a) Always happens because God desires it, and because it is fair and we deserve it

b) Does not always happen because God desires it

c) Does not always happen because it is fair and we deserve it

d) Happens because stuff happens

e) B & C

7. The "foil" for the truth found in the book of Job is:

a) Job's monologues

b) God's monologues

c) The advice of the comforters

d) B & C

8. At issue ultimately in reading Ecclesiastes — both in the case of the frame and also the Teacher's words — is to come to terms with the frequently used and very important Hebrew word *hebel*. What does this word mean?

a) Vanity

b) Meaningless

c) Futility

d) Vapor

e) All of the above

9. According to what theory does the bulk of Ecclesiastes represent a brilliant, artful argument for the way one would still find positive things to look at in life if God played a more distant role and if there were no life after death?

a) Wisdom theory

b) Vanity theory

c) Foil theory

d) Allegory theory

10. Although Song of Songs has had a long history of odd interpretation in the form of allegorizing, what is the book about?

a) God's love

b) Human love

c) The church's love

d) Christian love

CHAPTER 13

Revelation: Images of Judgment and Hope

You Should Know

- The taproot of apocalyptic literature is the Old Testament prophetic books.

- The primary meaning of Revelation is what John intended it to mean, which in turn must also have been something his readers could have understood it to mean.

- The key motif for the occasion and purpose of Revelation is "to those who are victorious."

- Chapters 1–3 set the stage and introduce most of the significant characters.

- Chapters 6–7; 8–11 begin the unfolding of the drama through three visions in structured sets of seven and reveal God's temporal judgment on Rome.

- Chapter 12 identifies the theological key to the book with two visions of Satan.

- Chapters 13–16 show how Satan's vengeance on the church took the form of the Roman Empire, but its emperors are doomed.

- Chapters 17–22 delineate a "tale of two cities" where the city of earth is condemned and then followed by the city of God where God's people dwell eternally.

- Nature of Revelation: apocalypse, prophecy, and letter

- Key distinction for interpreting Revelation: "tribulation" and "wrath"

Essay Questions

Short

1. The book of Revelation is a unique, finely blended combination of three distinct literary types: apocalypse, prophecy, and letter. Briefly summarize how Revelation reflects these literary types.

2. How is the motif "to those who are victorious" the key to understanding the historical context of Revelation, and how does it fully explain the occasion and purpose of the book?

3. In what way is Revelation much more like the epistles than the prophets? How are the hermeneutical difficulties with the book of Revelation much like those of the prophetic books?

Long

1. The book of Revelation unfolds like a great drama in which the earliest scenes set the stage and the cast of characters, and the later scenes presuppose all the earlier scenes and must be understood in order to follow the plot. Summarize each of the main sections of the book.

Quiz

1. As with most of the other biblical genres, the first key to the exegesis of the book of Revelation is to examine the kind of literature it is. Revelation is a unique, finely blended combination of three distinct literary types:

    a) Apocalypse, prophecy, and epistle
    b) Apocalypse, prophecy, and letter
    c) Apocalypse, narrative, and letter
    d) Apocalypse, prophecy, and narrative

2. The book of Revelation is primarily what kind of literature?

    a) Apocalypse
    b) Prophecy
    c) Letter
    d) Narrative

3. The book of Revelation fits all the common characteristics of apocalyptic literature from that era, but one:

a) Revelation is fantastical.
b) Revelation is literature.
c) Revelation is not pseudonymous.
d) Revelation is pseudonymous.

4. The combination of apocalyptic and prophetic elements in the book of Revelation has been cast in the form of:

a) A narrative
b) A letter
c) An epistle
d) A poem

5. The primary meaning of Revelation is found in:

a) What John intended it to mean
b) What John's readers could have understood it to mean
c) What we as readers understand it to mean
d) What interpreters believe it to mean
e) A & B

6. Any keys to interpreting the book of Revelation must be _____ to the text of Revelation itself or otherwise available to the original recipients from their own historical context. (p. 263–264)

a) Intrinsic
b) Implicit
c) Extrinsic
d) Explicit

7. One must have a sensitivity to the rich background of ideas that have gone into the composition of Revelation. What is the chief source of these ideas and images? (p. 264)

a) The Pentateuch
b) The narratives
c) The Old Testament
d) The Gospels

8. One of the keys for interpreting the book of Revelation is the distinction John makes between what two crucial words or ideas?

    a) "Tribulation" and "wrath"
    b) "Tribulation" and "rapture"
    c) "Perseverance" and "tribulation"
    d) "Perseverance" and "wrath"

9. Because the book of Revelation is a creatively structured whole and each vision is an integral part of that whole, one must think in:

    a) Oracles
    b) Paragraphs
    c) Sentences
    d) Pericopes

10. Which part is the theological key to the entire book of Revelation?

    a) Chapters 1–3
    b) Chapters 4–5
    c) Chapters 6–7
    d) Chapters 8–11
    e) Chapter 12
    f) Chapters 13–14

Notes